DATE DUE

Contents

R.L. 3.0 Spache Formula
ISBN: 531-09215-1
Library of Congress Catalog Card No. 83-60180

Published in 1983 by Warwick Press, 387 Park Avenue South
New York, New York 10016
First published 1982 by Kingfisher Books Ltd., London
Copyright © by Piper Books Ltd., 1982
Printed by Graficas Reunidas S.A., Madrid, Spain
5 4 3 2 1

PLANET EARTH

David Lambert

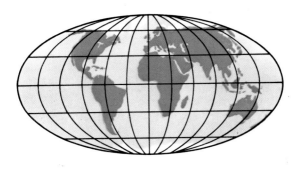

Editor: Jacqui Bailey
Series Design: David Jefferis

A Gateway Fact Book

Warwick Press
New York/London/Toronto/Sydney
1983

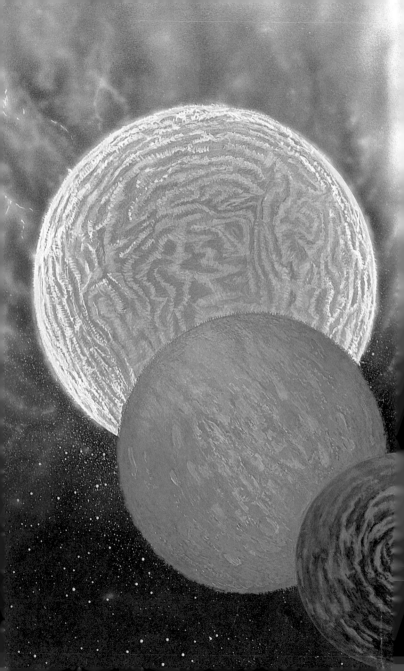

How Earth Began

At first there was no Earth. There was only a cloud of dusts and gases whirling through space. Then bits of matter in the cloud were drawn to each other. They stuck together and drew in other bits of ice and frozen gas mixed with rocks and minerals. By about 4.7 billion years ago they had formed a huge, whirling ball—the planet Earth.

Earth's Crust Is Formed

As the Earth spun it heated up. It became as hot as a glowing ember. The heaviest minerals sank to the center of the planet. Other, lighter matter rose to the surface. A thin crust formed, like the "skin" on chocolate pudding.

The Oceans Appear

From the boiling center of the Earth steam and hot gases escaped through the crust. They formed dark clouds covering the whole planet. Slowly the crust and the clouds cooled. Rain began to fall. The rain filled all the hollows in the Earth's crust. After millions of years these low areas became seas and oceans. The higher parts of the crust became islands and continents.

The Earth in Motion

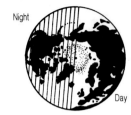

The Earth spins all the way around once every 24 hours.

The Earth is one of a group of nine planets. They travel in an oval path, or *orbit*, around a much larger star. We call this star the Sun. The Sun, its nine planets, and their moons form a *solar system*. But our solar system is just one of many. There are billions of stars in the star group, or *galaxy*, called the Milky Way.

The North Pole (N) starts to tilt toward the Sun after June 21. When the North Pole tilts toward the Sun it is summer in the north and winter in the south.

Days, Seasons, Years

It takes a year for the Earth to travel around the Sun. As it travels it also spins like a top. The north pole is at the head of this spinning "top" and the south pole is at the bottom. Each complete spin takes 24 hours—a day and a night. The Earth also tilts like a top. At times the northern part of the Earth is tilted toward the sun. It is then summer in the northern half of the world— the northern hemisphere. At the same time it is winter in the southern hemisphere.

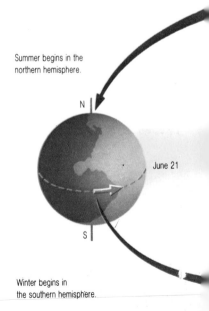

Summer begins in the northern hemisphere.

Winter begins in the southern hemisphere.

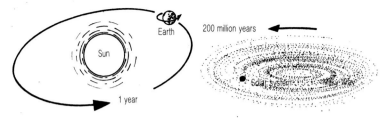

Once in 365¼ days the Earth orbits the Sun.

Once in 200 million years our solar system orbits the Milky Way.

The North Pole (N) tilts away from the Sun on December 21.

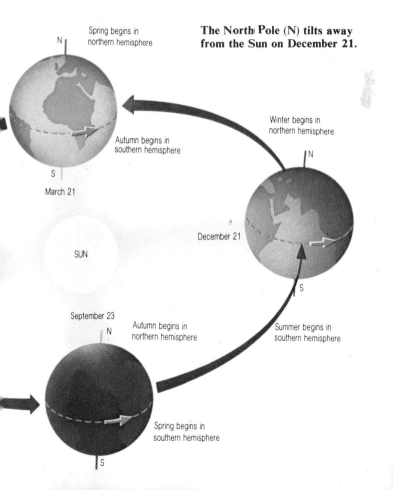

Spring begins in northern hemisphere

Autumn begins in southern hemisphere

March 21

SUN

Winter begins in northern hemisphere

December 21

Summer begins in southern hemisphere

September 23

Autumn begins in northern hemisphere

Spring begins in southern hemisphere

Inside the Earth

Until the space program began no one had seen our planet from space. Yet we knew what the Earth looked like—a giant beach ball. The ball is not perfectly round, however. It is slightly flattened at the poles. Around the middle, or equator, there is a bulge. Although no one has seen the inside of the Earth, we know a good deal about it. We know that it is nearly 4000 miles (6436 km) from the center of the Earth to the surface.

Shock Waves
So far, humans cannot travel through the Earth. But shock waves can. These waves are sometimes caused by earthquakes. Or they may be set off by man-made explosions. Scientists measure the speed at which shock waves travel through the Earth. By doing so they have learned that the Earth is made up of four different layers.

The Crust
The surface layer, or crust, is the thinnest. Below the oceans the crust is only about 5 miles (8 km) deep. It is about 20 miles (32 km) thick where there are continents.

Crust

Mantle

Inner core

Outer core

This diagram shows the Earth cut open. The three thick inner layers are shown, as well as the thin outer crust.

These deeper rocks are gray-green, and are rich in iron. The mantle is a thick, hot layer. Parts of it move slowly like sticky tar.

The Outer Core
Below the mantle lies a liquid shell of iron and nickle. This layer is called the outer core. It is around 1360 miles (2188 km) thick, and is extremely hot. Its heat is so intense that the metals in it have melted. They are liquid—like the molten lava from a volcano.

The Inner Core
Finally, at the very center of the Earth, there is an inner core. This central core is a solid ball of metal. It is about 1500 miles (2413 km) across. The inner core is the hottest part of our planet—as hot as the surface of the Sun. All the other layers press down on the Earth's inner core from above. Their weight helps to keep the inner core solid.

The Mantle
Just below the Earth's crust lies the mantle. The lighter rocks of the crust float on the heavier rocks of the mantle.

11

Restless Continents

The Earth has seven large land masses—the continents. They are scattered around the world. Seas and wide oceans separate them. But long ago they were probably joined together. Several clues show that this may be true. The east coasts of North and South America match the west coasts of Europe and Africa. If they were pushed toward each other they would fit together like pieces of a jigsaw puzzle. Rocks on the two coasts of the Atlantic Ocean also match each other. Plants and animals from continents that are far apart are very much alike. They seem to have come from the same families.

Shifting Plates

How could the continents drift apart? Scientists think they know the answer. The surface crust of the Earth floats on the mantle. The crust is made up of large slabs called "plates." Some plates carry the ocean floor. Some carry the continents. They all fit together, but not perfectly. Sometimes they shift about. Sometimes the plates are pushed apart by currents of molten rock. As the plates move, they carry whole continents or oceans with them.

300 million years ago

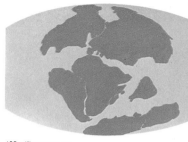

135 million years ago

The world today

These maps show how the continents may have shifted. About 300 million years ago they were bunched together. By 135 million years ago they were beginning to split up. Today the seven continents are widely scattered.

Below: (1) A current in the mantle (lying between Earth's crust and core) rises below an ocean floor. (2) Molten rock builds an underwater mountain ridge. (3) A cooling current sinks and drags the crust down into the mantle. Volcanic mountains are pushed up.

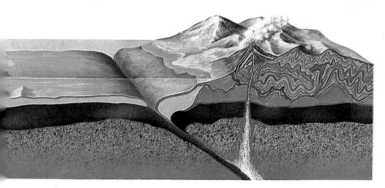

Earthquakes

The great plates that are part of the Earth's crust sometimes grind against each other. When they meet with a jerk, the land above them quakes and trembles. There is an earthquake. Huge cracks may appear in the Earth's surface. The land shifts. It rises or slips or sinks sideways. Buildings sway or fall as the land shifts under them.

Tsunami

Underwater earthquakes send out huge ocean waves. They are called *tsunami*. These waves travel across the open ocean at enormous speeds. Tsunami caused by an earthquake in the North Pacific can reach Hawaii, thousands of miles away, in a few hours. When tsunami near land they slow down. But they also rear up, like bucking broncos, towering over the shore. Tsunami sometimes go roaring inland, drowning villages and the people in them.

Earthquake Belts

Some parts of the world have more earthquakes than oth-

ers. They are called earth-quake belts. In the lands around the Pacific Ocean there are many earthquakes. Another earthquake belt runs from North Africa to China. Each year about half a million earthquakes are detected. Most of them do not cause much damage.

Recording earthquakes:
as the Earth trembles, a marker hanging from a spring draws a jagged line on a slowly turning drum.

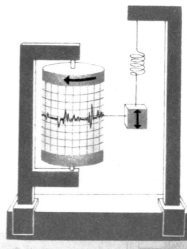

Below: in 1964 a great earth-quake hit Alaska. The ground shifted by more than 50 feet (15 m).

Volcanoes

Earthquakes and volcanoes occur at weak spots in the Earth's crust. In some areas the plates of the crust are shifting. They separate, or collide. These are the weakest spots in the Earth's crust. Many volcanoes are found in these areas.

Molten underground rock, or *magma*, forces up against the crust. It pushes with enough force to blast its way out. A volcano appears. In much the same way, boiling juice escapes through the crust of a baking pie.

Quiet Volcanoes

Some volcanoes quietly ooze hot, molten rock. This rock is called *lava*. If the lava is runny it spreads out over the land. Less runny lava builds a sloping cone around the hole, or vent, of the volcano. Sticky lava forms a tall, steep-sided cone.

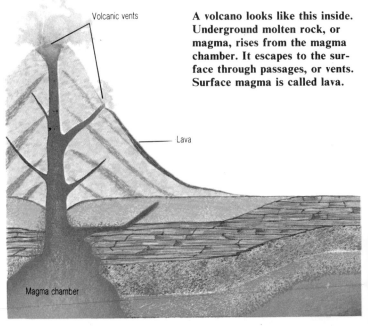

Volcanic vents

Lava

Magma chamber

A volcano looks like this inside. Underground molten rock, or magma, rises from the magma chamber. It escapes to the surface through passages, or vents. Surface magma is called lava.

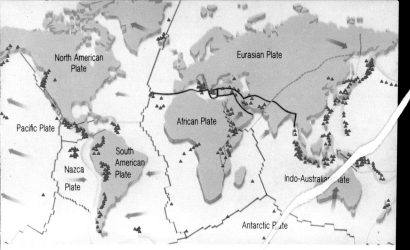

This map shows the plates of the Earth's crust and many of the 455 active land volcanoes.

→ Direction plate is moving
— Collision zone
▲ Volcano

Violent Volcanoes

Other, more violent volcanoes erupt like fireworks on the Fourth of July. Hot gas trapped underground presses on the rocks above. Finally they give way. Hot ash, cinders, and molten rock shoot up into the sky. Violent volcanoes build steep cones made of many layers of ash.

Dormant Volcanoes

Sometimes a volcano is quiet for centuries. But it may be merely dormant, which means "sleeping." Hot gas may be building up inside. This is exactly what happened in about 1470 B.C. A dormant volcano on the Greek island of Santorini erupted. When it blew up, the force was as great as that of hundreds of hydrogen bombs.

Extinct Volcanoes

Some volcanoes stop erupting for good. They are called extinct, or dead. Edinburgh Castle, in Scotland, stands on the remains of one such extinct volcano.

Mountains

When the plates of the Earth's crust collide mountains are thrust up.

The Himalayas

About 40 million years ago, India was an island. Then India and Asia collided. Between them lay a sea floor made of layers of rock. As Asia and India collided, the sea floor was forced up into huge humps called *fold mountains*. The result was the Himalayas—the highest range of mountains on the Earth. In the same way, the Alps were pushed up as Italy bumped into southern Europe.

The Rockies and Andes

North and South America also have fold mountains. But most of their highest peaks are volcanic. The Rocky Mountains and the Andes have risen where great plates meet. The west coast of the Americas actually rises over the edge of the great Pacific Plate. As we have seen (page 17), this is an area where many active volcanoes are found.

In 1980, Mount St. Helens, in Washington State, erupted causing enormous damage. Sixty-one people died, and the skies were clouded by volcanic ash for many months.

Block Mountains

Great cracks, called *faults*, sometimes appear in the Earth's crust. They, too, are caused by colliding plates. A block of land may be squeezed up between two

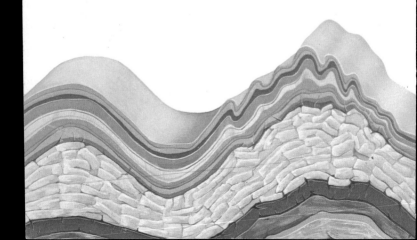

faults. It forms a flat-topped mountain called a *block mountain*. Europe's Vosges and Black Forest are block mountains.

Rift Valleys

Instead of rising, the land between two faults may sink. The sunken land is called a *rift valley*. The longest one on Earth runs through Africa.

Right: the sharply pointed Matterhorn is one of the European Alps.

Shifting plates cause rock layers to buckle (left), or to rise or sink (right).

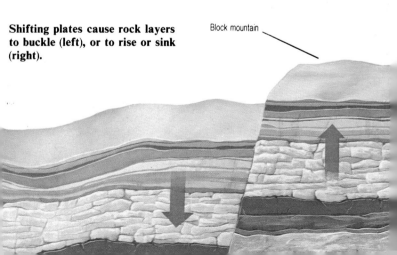

Block mountain

How Rocks Form

The Earth is a rocky planet. There are many kinds of rocks. But all of them come from the molten rock, or magma, which lies beneath the Earth's crust.

Igneous Rocks

Basalt, obsidian, and granite are all fiery, or *igneous*, rocks. Basalt and obsidian form when magma cools and hardens on the surface. Obsidian cools too fast for crystals to form. It is clear, like glass.

But granite is formed underground. It grows like giant blisters under the Earth's surface. The granite can be seen when other rocks above it have worn away. Because granite cools slowly, it forms crystals big enough for us to see.

The crystals found in rocks like granite are called *minerals*. There are about 2000 kinds of minerals.

Sedimentary Rocks

Some rocks are made from *sediments*. Sediments are loose bits of matter that have piled up on land or in water. When a pile of sediment becomes heavy enough, it squashes the bottom layer.

Then natural cements glue the squashed bits together. Solid rock, called *sedimentary rock*, is formed.

Most sedimentary rock—such as sandstone—is formed from small bits of igneous rock that has been broken up. But this is not true of limestone, another sedimentary rock. Limestone is made from the hard shells and skeletons of billions of tiny sea creatures.

Sedimentary rocks and sediments cover more than two-thirds of the Earth.

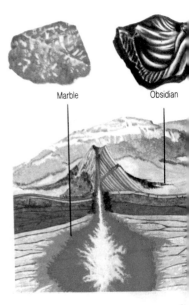

Marble

Obsidian

Metamorphic Rocks

Rocks sometimes change after they are formed. They turn into a new kind called *metamorphic* rock. What causes these changes? They are caused by high heat or enormous pressure.

A great mass of magma is pushed up through the Earth's crust. Rocks nearby are changed by the heat of the magma. Limestone changes into marble. Soft mudstone becomes hard slate. More heat changes the slate into mica-schist. And if things get still hotter, the mica-schist turns into an igneous rock called *gneiss* (pronounced "nice").

Rocks of the three main types: marble (metamorphic), obsidian and granite (igneous), limestone and conglomerate (sedimentary).

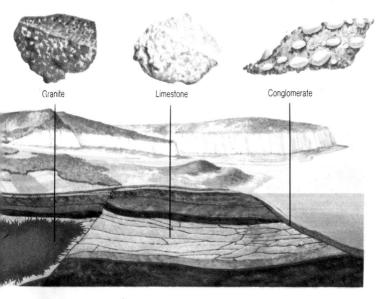

Granite   Limestone   Conglomerate

Effects of Weather

Rocks and mountains are slowly worn away by the weather. This takes a long, long time. It can take over 12,000 years to wear away just one yard (1 m) of soil and rock. Weather attacks the solid rock and breaks it up. Wind, rain, frost, and sunshine all join in this attack. They start by finding weak spots. Many rocks have loose particles. Some are cracked. Others are so soft that they can be dissolved by rain.

Heat and Cold

Heating and cooling break up lots of rock. In deserts it may be boiling hot in the daytime but cold at night. As rocks warm up they try to stretch. When they cool off they try to shrink. Strains occur inside the rock. In desert country, when night falls, there are sharp noises like a popgun. They

Above: flakes of loose rock on a mountainside

Left: limestone rocks worn bare by rain

are made by flakes of rock splitting off.

On cold, wet mountains ice breaks up rocks. Rainwater gathers in cracks in the rock. At night the water freezes. During the day it melts again. Each time ice forms it pushes against the sides of the rocks. In time, chunks of rock split off. They tumble down and form heaps of loose rock flakes called *scree*.

Powdery Rocks

Some kinds of rock slowly melt away when it rains. They are dissolved by water. Limestone rock may dissolve completely. In granite, only parts of the rock dissolve. Granite's feldspar crystals turn into a soft, powdery clay. But without feldspar to bind them the rest of the granite crystals drop away.

Rocks are also attacked by plants. The roots of plants creep into cracks in the rock. The roots make the cracks wider and wider. Sooner or later the rock is broken up. Even huge boulders have been broken up in this way. They are no match for the plants.

Landscape formed by a river:

(1) V-shaped valley

(2) Waterfall

(3) Gorge

(4) Meander

(5) Ox-bow lake

(6) Flood-plane

(7) Delta

Rivers at Work

Rivers carve out the land. They dig valleys and build islands. They also carry away rock. As soon as rock has been broken up, rivers start to carry it away. Each year they remove tons of rock and soil. Given enough time they can wear down the highest mountain range.

Mountain Streams

When it rains, water sinks down through the ground. In places it meets a layer of solid rock. The water can't sink any lower. Instead, it escapes by bubbling up as a spring. Many rivers begin as springs high up on mountainsides.

These springs feed streams. A mountain stream flows quickly downhill. As it goes it picks up bits of rock. The pieces of rock rub against the stream bed. Slowly they wear it away. The stream zig-zags downhill. It carves a narrow valley in the mountainside.

Tributaries

Small streams that join up with larger streams are called *tributaries*. They help the main stream grow. When the stream has grown big enough it becomes a river. From an airplane a river and its tributaries would look like the skeleton of a tree. The river is the trunk, and the tributaries are the branches.

The bits of rock carried downstream by the river break into smaller pieces. They grind against the river bed and against each other. Boulders become stones; stones form gravel; gravel turns to sand; and sand helps to make mud.

Lowland Rivers

When the river leaves the mountains it moves more slowly. Its bed becomes wider. The river flows lazily in wide loops. These loops are called *meanders*.

As the river reaches the sea, it dumps some of the sand and mud and gravel it has been carrying. This forms a fan-shaped area called a *delta* at the river mouth.

Underground Water

In limestone countryside underground caves are often found. They are carved out of limestone by water.

Clints and Grikes

A mass of limestone is made of giant blocks. The limestone blocks are called *clints*. They are packed closely together. But the limestone is full of tiny cracks between the clints. They run crosswise, and up and down.

Rainwater trickles into the surface cracks. It contains a little acid. The acid attacks the cracks and slowly makes them deeper. These deep cracks are called *grikes*.

Swallowholes

In time, some grikes become holes. These narrow holes lead straight down into the rock. Streams pour down them. Since the holes seem to swallow the streams, they are called *swallowholes*.

Caves

Water pouring down the swallowholes carves out caves. Some limestone caves are very big. Their ceilings are higher than our rooftops. The domed ceiling of one cave in France is 280 feet (85 m) high. Carlsbad Caverns, in

New Mexico, are even larger than that.

Inside the caves, *stalagmites* jut up from the floor. *Stalactites* hang from the ceiling, like icicles. But they are not made of ice. They are made of minerals. When a stalactite and a stalagmite meet, a pillar is formed.

A cave carved by water in a limestone mountain
(1) Clints and grikes
(2) Swallowholes
(3) Caves
(4) Stalagmites
(5) Stalactites
(6) Pillar

Ice Action

One-tenth of all the land on Earth lies buried under ice. Ice covers Antarctica and much of Greenland. These ice sheets are thick enough to cover any skyscraper. Years ago, they were even larger. Huge ice sheets covered much of North America and Europe.

Ice changes the shape of mountains. It may even grind them down to low stubs. Or it may carve out sharp peaks, called *horns*. Jagged ridges, known as *arêtes,* are also formed by ice.

Snowfields feed a small valley glacier.

Glaciers

Glaciers are slowly moving rivers made of ice. Snowfields high on mountainsides spill over into valleys. The tightly packed snow turns to ice. Loose bits of rock, picked up from the mountain, are frozen in the ice.

Glaciers creep along slowly. But as they move they scour the valley's floor and sides. The sharp bits of stone help to hollow out the valley.

Moraines

When a glacier melts, its rocks are left behind. Piles of rock dumped by glaciers are caled *moraines.*

The water from melting glaciers runs off in streams. The streams leave tracks behind them. The winding ridges they form are called *eskers.*

Oval humps of sand are also left behind by glaciers. These sandy hills are called *drumlins.* Bunker Hill, where one of the first battles of the American Revolution was fought, is a drumlin.

28

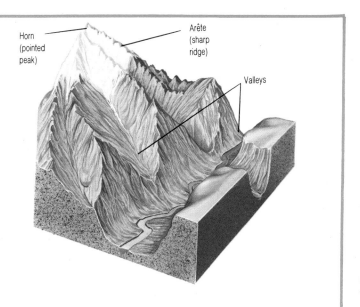

Above: valleys scooped out by glacier ice. Frost and ice have turned the peak of the mountain into a sharp horn, and formed jagged ridges, or *arêtes*.

Below: tracks left by a glacier. Moving ice has shaped the sandy, oval humps, called drumlins. Melting ice has left ridges, or eskers, of sand and gravel.

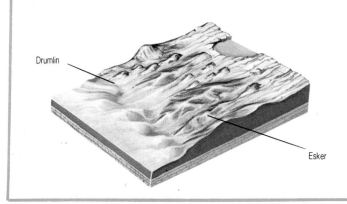

Desert Winds

A third of the world's land is desert. Desert land is too dry for plants. Bare rock surfaces and loose stone are open to attack by the wind. Winds move in and shape the desert.

Sand-blasting

Winds are not strong enough to move big stones. But they do pick up smaller bits of broken rock. They send gravel flying across the ground. They blow the sand waist high. And they send vast clouds of dust high into the sky.

Sand carves the rocks in the desert. Blown by the wind, it hits the rocks with stinging force. The sand carves out the soft rock. It can rub away the base of a huge boulder, until it falls over. Sand scoops out caves in cliffs of rock.

Left: windblown sand has carved away the base of this rock. Someday the boulder may topple.

Right: a long row of dunes in the desert sands.

Below: wind has curved the ends of this dune.

30

Seas of Sand

The Sahara Desert in Africa is the largest desert in the world. Here, windblown sand has scooped out a huge saucer. This immense hollow is called the Qattara Depression. It is lower than sea level, and larger than many whole countries.

Dunes

In some parts of the world, shifting winds cause the desert sands to lie in smooth sheets. But in other areas the wind always blows in the same direction. The sands pile up in *dunes*. A dune starts to grow when a rock or bush slows down the flow of the sand. As it grows, sands may blow across the top and down the other side. In time, this shifts the whole dune forward. Some deserts have row upon row of dunes. They inch forward so slowly that they look like frozen ocean waves.

Desert winds move sand from one place to another. They also carry thick layers of dust. Dust blown from the Gobi Desert covers large parts of China. Much of the soil in North America came from windblown dust.

Changing Shores

The shorelines of the world are always changing. Some coasts are being swiftly washed away by waves. Others are growing out into the sea.

Waves carve caves in each side of a cliff.

Shrinking Cliffs

Storm waves smash against the bottom of a cliff. They force air into narrow cracks in the rock. In time, the cracks widen. The blocks of rock between them become loose.

At last the rocks drop into the sea. Waves hurl them against the bottom of the cliff. More rock breaks off. The sea wears away the foot of the cliff and the cliff top falls. Bit by bit, the cliff moves back before the waves.

Soft rock is worn away much more quickly than harder rock. So bays are formed where there used to be soft rock. Between the bays, cliffs made of hard rock may remain standing. They are called *headlands*.

The caves meet, making an arch and a blowhole.

The top of the arch falls, leaving a rocky pillar.

Beaches and Mudflats

Ocean currents and waves carry bits of broken rock along the coast. In time, the rock bits become smaller and smaller. First they turn into gravel, then into sand, then into mud. They are washed up on the shore as sloping beaches.

Most beaches are in bays. But sand may also add a beach to a point of land jutting out into the water. Or a sandbar may build up across a narrow bay. If the sandbar becomes high enough it may cut the bay off from the sea. In this way a bay becomes landlocked.

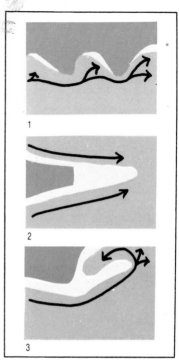

Above: three kinds of beaches are formed:
(1) Sand washed along a coast collects in bays.
(2) Sand builds a beach beyond a point of land.
(3) Sand builds a spit that juts out from a coast.

Left: a bar of sand and gravel has grown across a bay making a shallow lagoon.

Oceans and Seas

The salty waters of oceans and seas cover most of the Earth. Seas and oceans hold over thirty times more water than all the rivers, lakes, glaciers, ice, soil, and air combined. The oceans are the largest bodies of water. There are four of them, and they are all connected to each other.

The Pacific
The largest and deepest ocean is the Pacific. It is long enough and wide enough to swallow all the continents. Its deepest part is more than deep enough to swallow the world's highest mountain—Mount Everest.

The Atlantic
The second largest ocean is the Atlantic. It is less than half as big as the Pacific. Like the Pacific, it sprawls all the way from the Arctic to the Antarctic.

**Right: oceans hold 97%
of all water.**

**Below: water covers 71%
of the Earth.**

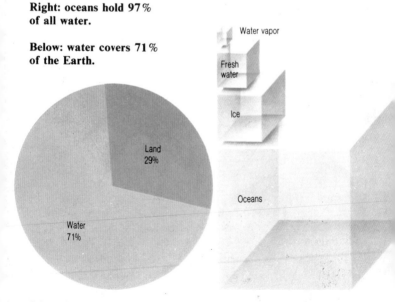

Water vapor

Fresh water

Ice

Oceans

Land
29%

Water
71%

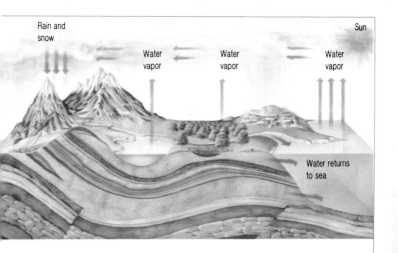

The Earth's Water Cycle: the Sun's heat sucks up water vapor from the sea and land.

Cooled vapor turns to rain or snow. It falls on the land and flows in rivers back to the sea.

The Indian Ocean
The third largest is the Indian Ocean. It is nearly as large as the Atlantic. It is also deeper than the Atlantic in most places.

The Arctic Ocean
This is the smallest and shallowest of the four great oceans. You could fit 13 Arctic Oceans into the Pacific and still have room to spare.

The Seas
Most seas are parts of oceans but are nearly cut off from them by land. The largest is the South China Sea—part of the Pacific Ocean. Some saltwater lakes are also known as seas. The Caspian Sea is the biggest of the inland seas.

Seawater

There is more to seawater than just a salty taste. And not all seawater is equally salty. Of the oceans, the saltiest is the Atlantic. The saltiest part of the Atlantic is the Sargasso Sea. This is a sunny area where lots of water is evaporated by the Sun. It is also far away from any rivers that would feed fresh water into it.

The Red Sea and the Persian Gulf have water that is even saltier. The Baltic Sea is the least salty. It is in a cool area with less sunshine. The Baltic is fed by many freshwater rivers and melting ice.

In salt water it is much easier to float because salt makes the water dense. This makes it fun for us to swim in it. It is also important to the animals that live in the sea.

Chemicals

In addition to sodium, or salt, there are many other chemicals in seawater. Most of them are present in very small amounts.

How do all these chemicals get into the ocean? Most of them probably come from weathered igneous rock.

A ship lowers instruments to study the ocean.

Some chemicals are washed into the ocean by rivers. Others dissolve from rocks in the ocean floor. And a few come from volcanic gases.

Temperature

Shallow waters near the equator are the hottest. The Persian Gulf sometimes gets as hot as 95°F (36°C) in the summertime. Oceans near the poles are frozen all year round. But deep water everywhere is cold. The average temperature for all depths of seawater all over the world is about 40°F (4°C).

Water Pressure

Near the surface of the ocean, the pressure of water is about the same as the pressure of the air. But the deeper you go, the greater it becomes. In the deepest parts of the Pacific, water pressure is a thousand times greater than at the surface. An ordinary submarine would be crushed to a pulp if it went this deep.

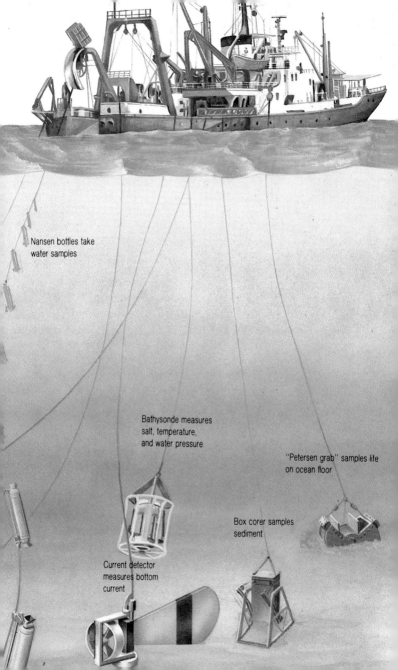

Nansen bottles take
water samples

Bathysonde measures
salt, temperature,
and water pressure

"Petersen grab" samples life
on ocean floor

Box corer samples
sediment

Current detector
measures bottom
current

Restless Oceans

The seas and oceans of the world are never still. They are always moving. Waves march across the oceans in rows. They are caused by the wind. Tides move in and move out on seashores. They are caused by the pull of the Moon and the Sun.

Waves

When the wind blows, waves start to move across the water. We can see them move. But the water itself does not travel with the wave.

To see how this happens, pick up a rope. Shake it. The rope will ripple. The ripples travel down the rope. But the rope itself does not move from your hand. Waves travel through water in the same way.

The crest, or tip, of each wave starts water particles moving. They circle up, down, and back up again. This motion at the surface causes the water below to start circling too. Below the crest of each wave is a stack of circling water.

As a wave nears land the water gets shallower. The lowest circles of water hit bottom. The wave slows down. Its crest rears up higher and higher. At last, the wave topples. It crashes on the beach with a mighty roar.

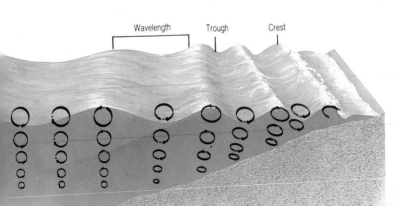

Wavelength   Trough   Crest

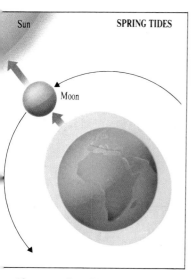

SPRING TIDES

Sun

Moon

Tides

The Moon travels around the Earth. Like the Earth, it has a gravitational pull. High tides happen as the pull of the moon and the spin of the Earth cause ocean water to pile up on opposite sides of the Earth. Low tides are the troughs that are left behind.

On all the world's seashores there are two high tides and two low tides each 24 hours. The ocean waters are always shifting.

Above: spring tides—Sun and Moon pull together.

Below: neap tides—they pull in different directions.

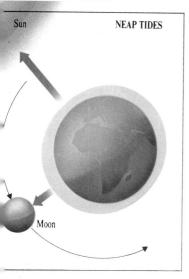

NEAP TIDES

Sun

Moon

Spring Tides

Tides are caused by the pull of the Moon. At times the Moon and the Sun both pull together. High tides are even higher than usual, and low tides are lower. These are all called *spring* tides.

Neap Tides

At other times the Sun and Moon pull in different directions. Then there are *neap* tides. The water rises and falls less than it usually does.

Ocean Currents

Currents are huge belts of water that flow like rivers through the world's oceans. Some ocean currents are bigger than the largest rivers. The West Wind Drift is one of them. It flows all the way around Antarctica. It carries 2000 times more water than the Amazon—the largest river in the world.

Winds start currents off. But when currents come to a continent, they must go around it. So they change directions. One odd thing about ocean currents is this: in the northern half of the world they are apt to flow to the right. In the southern hemisphere they flow to the left. This funny habit is caused by the Earth's spin.

OCEAN CURRENTS

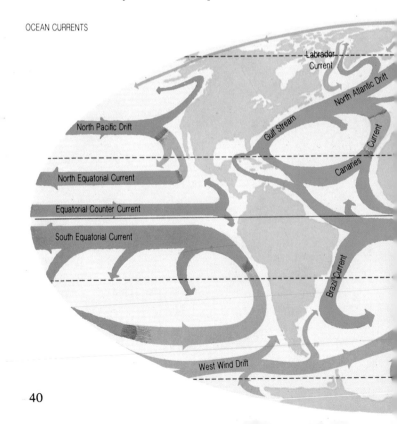

Rising and Sinking Water

Currents of icy water from the poles sink to the bottom. They flow along the ocean floor. When they reach the tropics, the cold water wells up to the surface. Water rising from the deep is rich in minerals. It helps feed ocean plants and animals.

Weather

Warm ocean currents heat the air above them. They warm nearby coasts. For example, Western Scotland has mild winters because the North Atlantic Drift keeps it warm. Eastern Canada has much colder winters. It is chilled by the Labrador Current. These two regions are equally close to the North Pole. But one is mild and the other is frigid as the result of two different ocean currents.

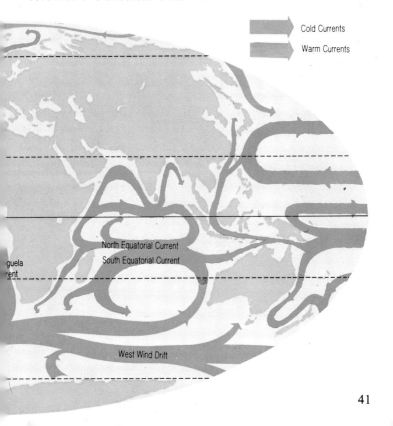

Cold Currents

Warm Currents

North Equatorial Current

South Equatorial Current

guela
ent

West Wind Drift

Ocean Depths

Suppose you are in a submarine. You are on your way across the Atlantic from Europe. The submarine is skimming along just above the ocean floor. What will you see along the way? You will see shelves and slopes.

First you cross a wide shelf called a *continental shelf*. Here the ocean is rather shallow. The shelf you are crossing is about 55 feet (17 m) deep. You reach the edge of the shelf. Ahead, the sea floor slopes steeply down. There are deep gashes in its sides.

Mountains and Trenches

At the bottom of the slope lie

Right: an underwater landscape

vast underwater plains. They are called *abyssal plains*. A chain of underwater mountains rises from them.

Finally, near Puerto Rico, the submarine plunges deeper. You have reached a narrow trench in the ocean floor. It is five miles (8 km) deep.

Trenches like this one are found in the Atlantic, the Pacific, and the Indian Oceans. The deepest of them are in the Pacific.

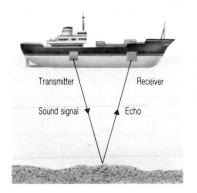

Transmitter

Receiver

Sound signal

Echo

Left: echo sounders find depths by measuring the time a sound takes to reach the bottom and echo back.

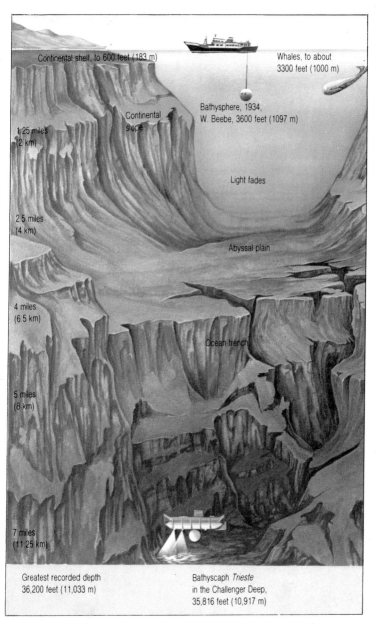

Continental shelf, to 600 feet (183 m)

Whales, to about 3300 feet (1000 m)

Continental slope

1.25 miles (2 km)

Bathysphere, 1934, W. Beebe, 3600 feet (1097 m)

Light fades

2.5 miles (4 km)

Abyssal plain

4 miles (6.5 km)

Ocean trench

5 miles (8 km)

7 miles (11.25 km)

Greatest recorded depth 36,200 feet (11,033 m)

Bathyscaph *Trieste* in the Challenger Deep, 35,816 feet (10,917 m)

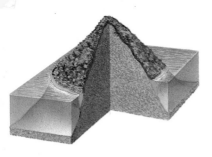

This volcanic island is rimmed by a stony reef of coral.

Islands

The world's oceans are dotted with islands. Greenland, the largest of them all, is almost four times the size of France. Others are so small that waves break over their tops.

Volcanic Islands

Many ocean islands have been built by volcanoes. They sometimes appear very suddenly. One day there is open sea. Next day, the sea begins to boil. Within a few days the smoking tip of a volcano emerges from the waves. In a matter of weeks, a new island has been born.

The volcano is sinking but the coral keeps on growing upward.

There are many volcanic islands in the Atlantic. They rise from a crack in the ocean floor. The crack runs down the middle of the Mid-Atlantic Ridge.

The Pacific Ocean also has thousands of volcanic islands. Many now lie beneath the surface. In some cases their tops have been worn down by waves. They are now underwater mountains. In other cases the volcano has left a coral atoll behind.

The volcanic island has sunk, leaving only the coral reef, called an atoll.

Island Arcs

Curving rows of islands are called *island arcs*. Japan, Sumatra, Java, and New Zealand all belong to island arcs. Most of these islands are *fold mountains*. They were thrust up when two of the Earth's great plates collided. Island arcs also have some volcanic islands.

Continental Islands

Some islands were once parts of continents. They are called *continental islands*. At some time in the past, the level of the sea rose. The islands were cut off from the mainland.

The Florida Keys are low, sandy islands.

Great Britain and Ireland were once part of continental Europe. Stretches of low land connected them to the continent. The connecting land is still there: But it has been covered by the sea.

In the past, Borneo, Java, and Sumatra were part of southeast Asia. Then the sea rose and cut them off from the mainland. They are now separated by miles of open seas and oceans.

The Atmosphere

The Earth is surrounded by a thin skin of gases. It is called the *atmosphere*. Our atmosphere is made up of mixed gases, mostly nitrogen and oxygen. Without them there would be no living things. In our air are tiny amounts of other gases. The air also contains water vapor and dust.

The Layers of Atmosphere

There are five layers of atmosphere. The layer we live in is called the *troposphere*. It is a thin layer—5 to 10 miles (8-16 km) deep. It gets colder as you rise through the air of the troposphere.

The second layer is the *stratosphere*. This layer contains ozone. Ozone is a kind of oxygen. It helps shut out harmful rays from the Sun.

Above the stratosphere lies the *mesosphere*. This is the coldest part of the atmosphere.

The next layer is the *ionosphere*. It is about 250 miles (400 km) deep.

The outer layer is called the *exosphere*. It is made of thinly scattered gases that stretch far out into space.

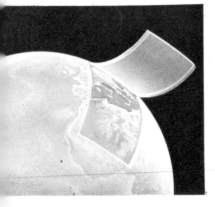

Left: air is a thin skin of gases clinging to the Earth's surface.

Right: the five layers of the Earth's atmosphere. In or above the stratosphere meteors burn up. In the ionosphere, solar particles make colored lights called auroras.

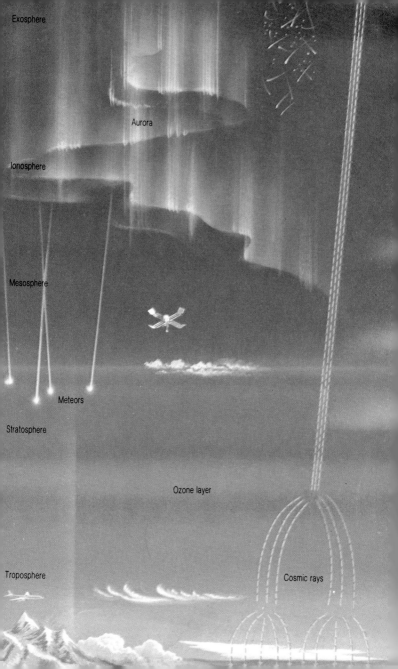

Exosphere

Aurora

Ionosphere

Mesosphere

Meteors

Stratosphere

Ozone layer

Troposphere

Cosmic rays

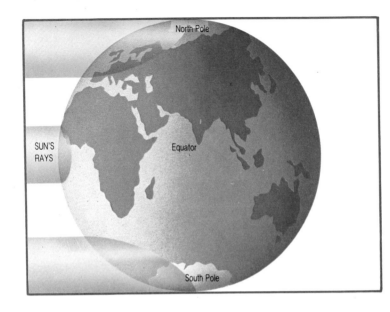

North Pole

SUN'S
RAYS

Equator

South Pole

Sun and Wind

The Sun keeps our planet warm. Its energy is beamed down to the Earth. Rays of sunlight are trapped by the air. Wind spreads that heat around the world.

Lost Sunshine

Only about half of the energy sent in our direction reaches the Earth's surface. Some of it is stopped by the outer layers of the atmosphere. One-third of it is bounced back into space. The Sun's rays bounce off bits of dust or water vapor in the air. Blue light is scattered the most. That is why the sky seems blue.

Some of the Sun's energy does reach us. It is enough to heat up the world's continents and oceans. The land and sea are warmed by the rays of the Sun. In turn they help to warm the air above them.

Nature's Greenhouse

The Earth is a little like a greenhouse. The air is the greenhouse roof. It lets in the warmth of the Sun. But it also keeps the heat from escaping.

What would the world be like without our roof of air? It would be much colder at night and in winter. Air helps us keep warm even when the Sun isn't shining.

The World's Winds

When air is hot it rises. Cool air grows heavy and sinks.

Rising and falling air starts winds moving.

Near the equator, warm air rises. It flows north and south. As it cools it grows heavy and sinks. At the poles, cold air flows toward the equator. Winds are also affected by the spinning of the Earth beneath them. It makes winds veer off in new directions.

Below: trade winds are warm. Westerlies are cooler. Polar Easterlies are coldest of all.

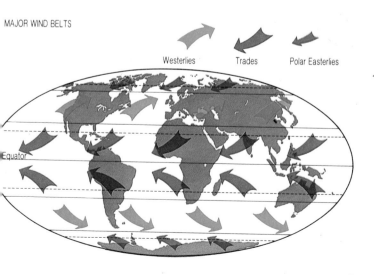

MAJOR WIND BELTS

Westerlies   Trades   Polar Easterlies

Equator

Climate

Climate is the pattern of weather in an area. The pattern is made up of all kinds of weather. The amount of sunshine, rain, snow, frost, and wind in any area makes its climate.

Hot and Cold

The hottest climates on Earth are in the tropics. The tropics are regions near the equator. There the Sun shines most directly on the surface of the land.

The coldest climates are near the poles. In the Arctic and Antarctic there are some days when the Sun does not rise at all. The amount of sunshine is small.

Between the tropics and the polar lands lie areas with *temperate* climates. They have warm summers and cool

In the Arctic, winter lasts nine months. People and goods may travel by dogsled.

Huts with roofs of palm fronds are shelter enough in the warm tropics.

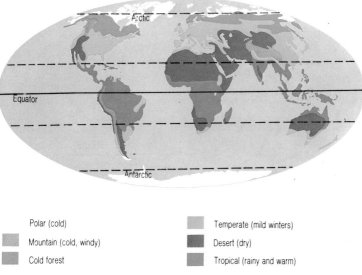

Polar (cold)

Mountain (cold, windy)

Cold forest

Temperate (mild winters)

Desert (dry)

Tropical (rainy and warm)

winters. We call these areas the temperate zones.

Climate is affected in many ways. Ocean currents warm or cool the seacoasts. Polar winds chill the land. Tropical winds make it warmer.

Mountain ranges may protect an area from icy polar winds. But mountaintops are always cold. This is true even in the tropics. The Andes Mountains of South America lie near the equator. But they are capped with snow.

Wet and Dry

Some of the rain in temperate areas comes all the way from the tropics. It is carried by the winds.

The Sun sucks up lots of water from tropic seas. This vapor cools as it rises. When moist air cools, the water vapor turns to raindrops. The raindrops are too heavy to float in the clouds. Rain begins to fall.

Air that blows over the oceans is moist. The air of inland places is apt to be much drier. Because of this the coast usually has more rain than inland areas.

51

Weather

Depressions

Near the equator the weather follows the same pattern year round. In Malaysia the morning is almost always bright and sunny. The afternoon is cloudy and wet. The temperature is near 80°F (27°C) all year.

The weather in temperate regions changes often. A cool, rainy morning may be followed by a warm and sunny afternoon. That night there may be frost, with gale winds and rain the next day.

Why does the weather change so much in the temperate zone? The winds are the cause.

When warm air from the tropics meets cold polar air a *depression* is formed. Depressions are whirling masses of warm and cold air. They are hundreds of miles wide.

In a depression in the southern hemisphere winds blow around clockwise. In the northern hemisphere they blow the other way.

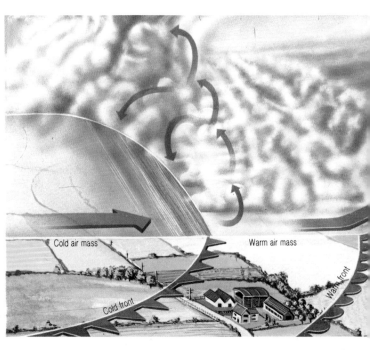

Cold air mass   Warm air mass

Cold front   Warm front

Weather Fronts

The front edge of a mass of cold air is called a *cold front*. A *warm front* is the edge of a warm air mass.

Inside a depression, warm air rises. It is pushed up by the heavy cold air under it. As it rises it cools. Drops of water form and build clouds. It starts to rain.

So depressions bring rain and windy weather. They form in temperate areas since that is where cold polar air and warm tropic air meet.

The weather changes often.

In some areas there is a saying, "If you don't like the weather, wait a minute."

A depression moving from left to right.

Warm air rises, cools, and sheds rain. Rain falls ahead of the warm front and behind the cold front.

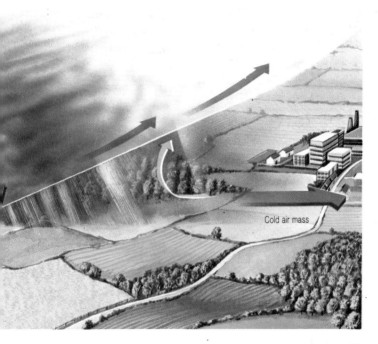

Cold air mass

53

Living Things

Life began more than 3500 million years ago. The first living things were tiny creatures floating in the sea. In time these sea creatures became larger nd less simple. By 600 million years ago there were mar , types. Sea worms burrowed into the sea bed. Broad, flat trilobites crawled around on jointed legs.

Amphibians

By 500 million years ago, wormlike animals were becoming fish. They were the first creatures with backbones. Some fish developed lungs and fins. They began to spend part of their time on land. Next came frogs and other amphibians. Amphibians are animals who live on land but lay their eggs in the water. They were among the first living creatures that moved onto the land.

Fossils of animals and plants:
(1) Mold and cast of a trilobite.
(2) Petrified wood.
(3) Prehistoric fern.
(4) Fossil teeth.
(5) Footprints in mud, now turned to stone.

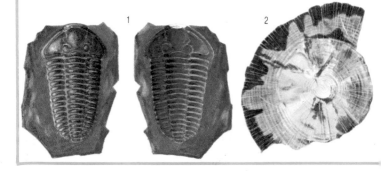

Amphibians led to reptiles like snakes and lizards. By 150 million years ago there were mammals and birds.

Fossils

Many of the first kinds of living things have died out. They are extinct. But we know what some of them were like. They have left fossils behind.

Fossils are traces left in rock by something that has died. A fossil may form if a dead animal or plant sinks to a muddy seabed. It is protected by mud piled up around it. As it slowly dissolves its hard parts are replaced by minerals. Then the mud turns to rock with the fossil locked inside.

Rocks with fossils in them may be pushed above the sea. Weather may wear away the surface of the rock. Or the rock may be split apart. Then the fossil appears, and we know what the early creature was like.

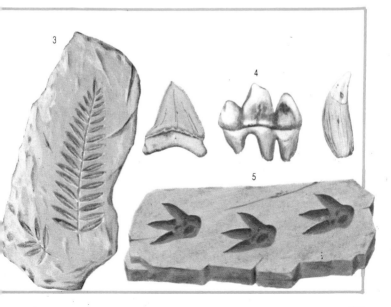

Soil

Soil is more valuable than anything else on land. Nearly all of our food comes from the soil.

The soil lies on the surface in a thin layer. Under it are the rocks of the Earth's crust. But without this thin cover of soil, plants would not grow. Without plants to eat, animals would starve. The plants and animals that we live on would disappear.

Plants and Soil

Soil helps plants in several ways. It provides them with a foothold. Plants firmly rooted in the soil do not wash away or blow away.

Soil also holds moisture and food that plants suck up with their roots.

Finally, the soil stores heat. This helps plants to grow. The heat of the soil is especially important in spring and fall. When the air cools at night the soil keeps plants warm.

Soil Layers

Most soil has three layers. The top layer is full of *humus*. Humus is decayed plant and animal material. It is full of plant food.

Rain washes plant food deep into the soil in this cool, wet forest area.

The second layer is humus mixed with sand and gravel. The last layer is broken rock.

Types of Soil

Some soils are light and sandy. Water drains through them rapidly. Loamy soils are rich in humus. Clay soils are dense and heavy. Water stays in them instead of running off.

Soil type depends partly on

Grassland soil gets little rain. Plant food stays near the surface.

Water evaporating from desert soil leaves a salty crust. Few plants grow.

the rocks beneath the ground. But climate has a greater effect.

Climate and Soil

Tundra soils of the north have a layer of peat (made from rotted moss) on top. Then comes a layer of mud. Below that the soil is frozen all year around.

Huge dryish areas of North America and Russia have a rich soil called black earth.

Rainy tropical climates have brick-red soils. Heavy rains wash the humus deep into them.

Hot deserts have reddish brown soils. Salts sucked up by heat lie on the surface.

The brown forest soils of western Europe are rich in humus. It is made from the rotted leaves of forest trees.

Plants

Above: cactuses hold moisture. They thrive in deserts.

Below: banana plants need a warm, damp climate.

The world can be divided into natural regions. Each has its own set of plants.

Plants of the North

In the cold, far north lies a region called the tundra. Only lichens, mosses, flowers, and small shrubs grow here. Frost and cold winds would kill other plants.

South of the tundra lies a huge belt of conifer, or pine, forest. Conifers are able to survive long, cold winters.

Right: a climb up a tall peak at the equator takes you though many plant zones.

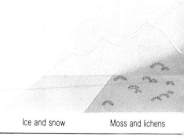

Ice and snow　　Moss and lichens

Farther south are the deciduous forests. The deciduous trees, such as oaks and beeches, shed their leaves in winter.

In the dry lands of eastern Europe short grasses take the place of forest trees. These lands are called steppes.

Plants of Warm Lands

Around the Mediterranean the summers are long, hot, and dry. The trees and shrubs have tough leaves that keep the plants from drying up.

To the south sprawls the Sahara Desert. It is always hot and dry. Some desert plants have thorny leaves. They hold water and keep animals away.

South of the Sahara is the savanna. Tall grasses and scattered trees grow here.

At the equator there are tropical rain forests. The broad leaves of tall trees meet high above the dark floor of the forest.

Mountain Plants

If you climbed a mountain in the tropics you would go through many natural regions. It would get colder and colder as you climbed higher. At the top of the mountain you would find plants much like those that grow in the Arctic.

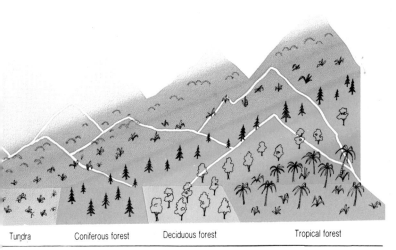

| Tundra | Coniferous forest | Deciduous forest | Tropical forest |

Animals

Some groups of animals are kept apart by oceans, mountains, or deserts. For millions of years they have lived away from other groups. They become different from the rest.

The world has six main animal regions. Each has its own set of wild animals that are not found anywhere else.

Northern Regions

Only the *Nearctic Region* of North America has the pronghorn antelope, the bowfin (a freshwater fish), and certain families of lizards.

Hedge sparrows are found only in the *Palaearctic Region*. This region covers Europe and much of Asia.

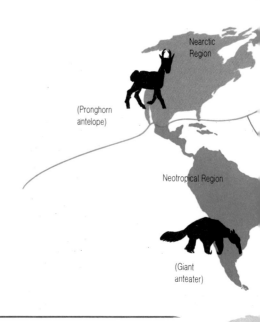

Animal regions of the world:
the pronghorn antelope, hippopotamus, kangaroo, and giant anteater each live in a separate region. They have no close relatives among the animals of other regions. But the horse and the Indian elephant are related to some animals of Ethiopia.

Nearctic Region

(Pronghorn antelope)

Neotropical Region

(Giant anteater)

Southern Regions

The *Ethiopian Region* lies mainly in Africa. It is the only home of the hippopotamus, the hyrax and the ostrich.

Southern Asia, called the *Oriental Region*, also has animals that are not found anywhere else on Earth. They include the flying lemur, the tree shrew, and fairy bluebirds.

South America was once cut off from North America. Because of this the *Neotropical Region* has many unusual wild animals. Among them are anteaters, New World monkeys, and sloths.

In the *Australian Region*, or *Australasia*, we find the strangest animals of all. The platypus and the echidna are the only mammals in the world that lay eggs. This is also the home of the kangaroo, the koala bear, and the wombat. They are all marsupials. Marsupials are mammals. The female has a pocket on her belly where she carries her tiny young.

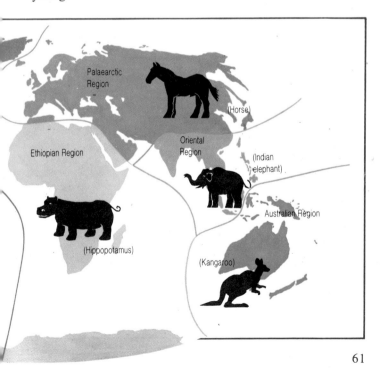

Palaearctic Region

(Horse)

Oriental Region

Ethiopian Region

(Indian elephant)

Australian Region

(Hippopotamus)

(Kangaroo)

Peoples of the World

How many people live on the Earth? There are more than 4000 million of us.

People come in many different sizes, shapes, and colors. Those who lived in areas with hot climates became darker than people in cold regions. Brown skins helped protect them from harmful rays of the tropic Sun. In the north, the sunlight was weak. Pale skin helped the people living there. In the same way, short arms and legs were best in the cold parts of northern Asia. The blood did not have so far to travel.

People of all kinds and colors have now spread around the world. Many Africans live in Europe and in North and South America. And many Europeans live in Africa. Most of the people who live in Australia and New Zealand come from European settlers. Chinese and Indian people have made new homes in many lands.

Above: a Chinese girl

Left: Spanish-Americans at a street market

Above: women of Sri Lanka at work in a field

Today many people have relatives from different racial and national groups. An American child may have a mother who is Japanese and a father who is Italian.

Other Differences

Color is one of the least of the differences between people. There are nearly 3000 different spoken languages. Most of us speak only one or two. We cannot understand the others. This is sometimes true even of people living in the same country. In India 14 different languages are spoken. There is no one language that everyone understands.

People also believe in different gods. There are 11 main religions in the world. This is another difference that sometimes keeps people apart.

Groups of people form nations. The world has more than 160 nations. And as we know, nations may go to war.

These are some of the differences that divide people and keep them from living together in peace.

Wealth from the Soil

Early people were hunters. They killed animals for meat. They gathered roots and berries to eat.

Then, about 8000 years ago people started to grow crops. Instead of killing animals they tamed and raised them.

Farming spread around the world. There was more food. As fewer people starved the number of people grew.

Farmers settled down in villages. They grew more food than they needed to eat. Extra food was traded to others. Some people learned crafts or became traders.

Farming villages grew into towns and even cities. Today, few of us grow all the food we eat. We depend on farmers for our food.

Plants

One-tenth of all land is used for growing crops. It is called *arable* land.

Two-thirds of all arable land grows cereals: grains such as barley, wheat, and rice. Fruits, vegetables, and oil-producing plants (such as olive trees) are also grown.

We don't eat cotton or rubber. They are grown to give us other things we need.

Forests provide timber. Soft wood from northern forests is used for making paper. Hardwood trees from warmer areas are used for building. Their wood also goes into furniture making.

Animals

One-fifth of all land is used as pasture. Animals such as cows, chickens, and goats are raised. Farm animals give us meat, eggs, and milk. Wool and animal skins are used for clothing.

Right: oxen plow rice fields in India.

Inset: wheat is cut on the grasslands of North America.

Riches from Rocks

The food we eat comes from soil and water. But many other things we use come from rocks.

Tools, machines, cars—even pots and pans—are made of metal. And the metal comes from rocks under the ground.

Some rocks are rich in mineral *ores*. Ores contain metals. Iron, copper, tin, lead, and zinc are among the metals we get from ores.

Hunting for Ores

Ore deposits are scattered around the world. Finding them is not easy.

Geologists use special tools in hunting for ore. Magnetometers help in finding iron. Geiger counters discover uranium. Gravimeters and seismographs are other tools. They help build up a picture of the rock layers deep underground.

Right: a factory turns out new cars. The metal used to make cars comes from rocks.

Mining

Ores near the surface are easy to remove. Iron and copper ores are scooped out of open pits. The work is done by giant power shovels. Huge holes and piles of rubble are often left behind.

Other mineral ores lie deep below the ground. Miners may have to tunnel through solid rock to reach them. One gold mine in South Africa goes down for almost 2½ miles (4 km).

Refineries and Factories

After ores have been dug up, the metal must be separated from the rest of the ore. This is called "refining." Iron ore is refined by heating it in a blast furnace. The iron melts and is poured off. As it cools it hardens into strong iron.

Left: an open-pit iron-ore mine in Australia. The ore is removed by machines.

The final step is to shape the metal. This is done in factories that make everything from cars to kettles. The metal they are made of came from rocks beneath the ground.

Fuel and Power

Energy to work comes from the food we eat. Early people did all the work themselves.

Today, we have machines and engines. They are more powerful than any human body. Some of them lift and move heavy loads. Others light and heat whole cities. Many engines get energy from fossil fuels.

Fossil Fuels

Coal, oil, and natural gas are fossil fuels. They were formed many millions of years ago. These fuels come from the remains of living things buried beneath the ground.

Coal is the remains of prehistoric trees. They grew about 300 million years ago. Thick layers of dead trees were drowned by the sea. Then they were crushed by layers of mud and sand. This pressure helped to change them from wood into coal.

Oil and natural gas come from the remains of tiny animals and plants that lived in shallow warm seas. Then the Earth's crust shifted, and they were trapped under rocks. In time, they turned into oil or gas.

Miners get some coal from open pits on the Earth's surface. Underground mines give us more coal.

Oil and gas come from wells. These are holes cut deep into the Earth's crust. Some of them go down a long way. One gas well is almost 6 miles (9.5 km) deep.

Left: machines biting through solid rock cut coal deep under the ground.

Water Power

Some rivers and waterfalls run very swiftly. Their water can spin huge wheels, called turbines. The turbines make electricity, which we use in many ways.

Nuclear Energy

We mine uranium ore to produce nuclear energy. Huge amounts of energy are released by splitting the atoms that make up uranium.

Above: burning off waste gas above a gas field

Below: the diagram compares the amounts of fuels used to supply the world's energy from 1830 to 1970. Now we use even more oil and gas. Some day it will all be gone.

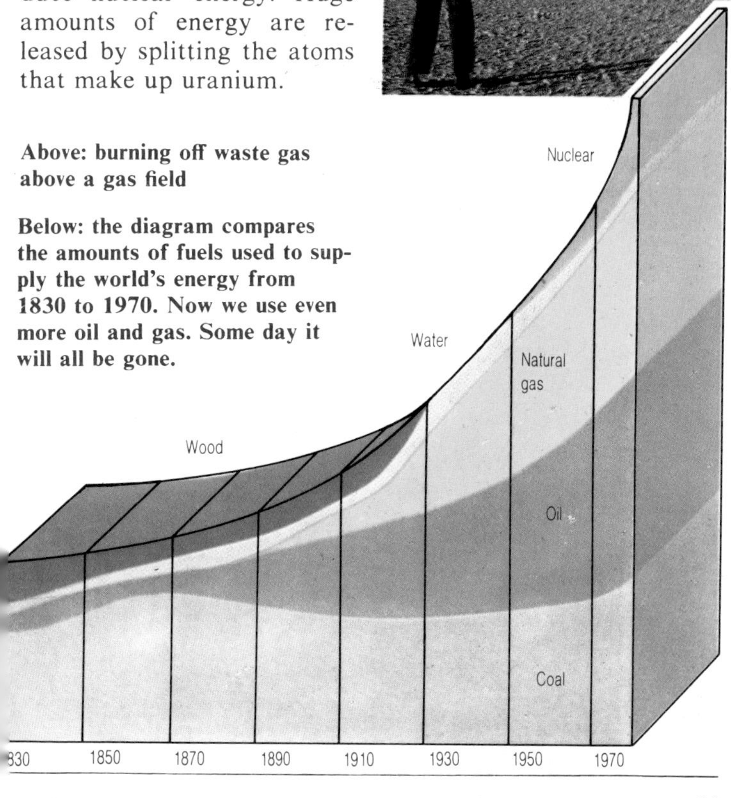

Nuclear

Water

Wood

Natural gas

Oil

Coal

830   1850   1870   1890   1910   1930   1950   1970

69

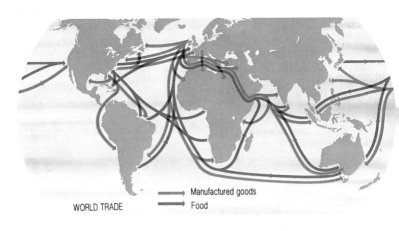

WORLD TRADE → Manufactured goods
→ Food

Trade and Transport

Some nations have more of certain goods than they need.
They sell the extra goods to other countries. Then they buy
the things they lack. As a result, vast amounts of food, raw
materials such as minerals, and manufactured goods travel
around the world. Services like banking, insurance, and
tourism also count as exports or imports.

Buying and Selling

The goods that a nation sells to other countries are called
exports. The goods that it buys are imports.

Some countries buy and sell more than others. The major
trading nations are the United States, West Germany, and
Japan. They sell the goods made by their many factories.
They buy fuel and other materials to keep those factories
busy. Great Britain exports a third of what it makes. It
imports half of its food and raw material.

Poorer countries have fewer factories. So they import
manufactured goods. They sell food and raw materials. For
example, countries like Colombia and Ghana supply the rest
of the world with coffee and cocoa.

Left: this map shows
the world's trade flow.

Right: donkey transport
in Syria

Below: goods packed in
containers go by land
and sea.

How Goods Travel

Vast amounts of goods are sent all over the world by land,
air, and sea. On land, heavy loads like coal and steel go by
train. Lighter goods are moved by truck. Oil, natural gas,
and water travel through pipelines.

Fleets of tankers and container ships move goods by sea.
Water transport is the slowest way of getting from one place
to another. But it also costs less than other means. Air transport is the most costly. It is also the fastest. Planes mainly
carry passengers and mail.

How People Live

Modern farming, mining, and machinery have changed the lives of people in some parts of the world.

With new ways of farming, three or four farm workers can grow enough food to feed 100 people. Fewer people need to work as farmers. Instead many may work in mines or factories. Or their jobs may be in schools, hospitals, offices, or shops.

These newer jobs bring people into towns and cities. The cities grow larger. Tokyo and Mexico City now have about 10 million people each. Many other cities are growing fast.

Haves and Have Nots

Some people live much easier lives than others. Developed countries can make life better for most of their people. In some parts of the world many families have homes, cars, and television sets. They even have dishwashers and vacuum cleaners to save work.

Life is harsh in the world's poorer countries. In China, eight out of every ten people must work on farms in order to feed themselves.

In some areas, people are too poor to see a doctor if they become ill. Millions of people do not have enough food to eat. Many die very young.

More and More People

The number of people in the world is growing every year. It has more than doubled since 1930. By 2020 it may have doubled again.

In poor countries the number of people grows the fastest. These countries already have too little food. And they are the least able to use modern ways of farming. Many experts are studying ways to grow more food. Others are helping people plan families with fewer children.

Rich and poor live side by side in Rio de Janeiro, Brazil.

A Crowded Planet

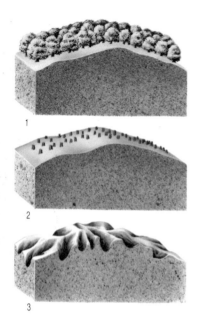

As the number of people on the Earth grows, more of everything is needed. More people need more food, more water, more lumber, more minerals. In the process of taking all these things from the Earth we have damaged our planet.

Damage to the Earth

People need roads, mines, and cities. They drain swamps, cut down forests, and destroy topsoil. Land, air, water, and living things all suffer.

When a swamp or forest is destroyed, the animals that live there die. When the soil is robbed of plant food, the plants die and the soil itself may be washed or blown away. When wastes pour into lakes, rivers, and seas, water plants and animals are killed. We are hurting our planet in all these ways. If the number of people on Earth keeps growing, we may soon use up

Above: damage to forestland.
(1) A healthy forestland bound by tree roots.
(2) Trees are cut, soil loses nourishment.
(3) Rain has washed soil away.

Left: using scrap metal from dumps like this can save minerals.

many minerals. The fossil fuels we depend on for energy may also run out.

The biggest danger is that nations may go to war over these scarce materials. If they fight with nuclear bombs, all living things will die.

Saving the Earth

Many things can be done to help. Land set aside as nature parks keeps wild animals and plants alive. The soil can be helped by careful farming and forestry. Laws can be passed to help safeguard the air and water.

Scarce minerals can be saved by using scrap metal over again. New ways to use wind and water for energy might save on fossil fuels.

But our main need is to limit the very rapid growth in the number of people living on the Earth.

Above: oil spills at sea kill seabirds.

Right: a nuclear bomb blast could kill all life on Earth.

Surprising Facts

Natural Wonders

The places described on these pages are among the greatest natural wonders of the world.

A Mushroom Mountain

One day in 1943, a Mexican farmer named Dionisio Pulido was working in his field. He heard a sound like thunder. Smoke began rising from the ground. It was the start of a volcano. The ground gaped open. Hot cinders started flying from the hole.

The next day most of his farm was covered by 15 feet (5 m) of black lava. By nightfall the volcano was 150 feet (46 m) high.

The volcano grew. It buried the nearby village of Parícutin in ash. Then lava flowed several miles further. It swallowed another village. By the time Mount Parícutin stopped growing it stood 8200 feet (2500 m) high. Since 1952 Parícutin has been quiet.

Approximate height
1250 ft (380 m)

328 ft (100 m)

Rainbow Bridge

The longest and largest natural arch in the world is in southern Utah. It has two names. The Navajos call it Nonesonshi. It is commonly called Rainbow Bridge.

It was carved out of limestone by running water. Long ago a looping river cut caves in opposite sides of a cliff. It hollowed out the caves until they met. The cliff top above became a narrow bridge.

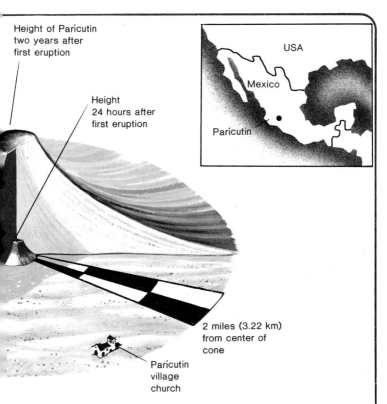

Height of Parícutin
two years after
first eruption

Height
24 hours after
first eruption

USA

Mexico

Parícutin

2 miles (3.22 km)
from center of
cone

Parícutin
village
church

Grand Canyon

It took the Colorado River about a million years to carve the Grand Canyon. It is in Arizona. The gorge, which is the world's largest, is a mile (1.6 km) deep and averages 8 miles (13 km) wide.

The steep walls form a diary of the Earth's past. They are full of fossils and footprints of ancient creatures. Layer after layer came to light as the river deepened its bed.

Exploring the World

It took thousands of years for Stone Age people to spread around the world. Today, satellites are able to circle the Earth in hours.

Stone Age Seafarers

Three thousand years ago Stone Age farmers began sailing out into the ocean. They made new homes on the islands of the Pacific. Their boats were canoes or catamarans. An early catamaran (inset) was two canoes lashed together. Between them was a platform. It sometimes held a hut for shelter.

Early seafarers followed ocean currents. Birds and stars helped guide them. In time they settled on many far-flung islands in the Pacific Ocean. We now call these islands Polynesia.

Spy in the Sky

The first maps were made by measuring the land. This was slow work. It took hundreds of years. Today the work is done by satellites. Their cameras photograph the Earth constantly.

Landsats, like the one shown (right), have orbited the Earth. Their cameras photograph areas too wild to be explored.

Pictures taken by satellite also help in other ways. They show where crops have been damaged. And sometimes they help geologists discover new mineral deposits.

Landsat (above)

Catamaran (below)

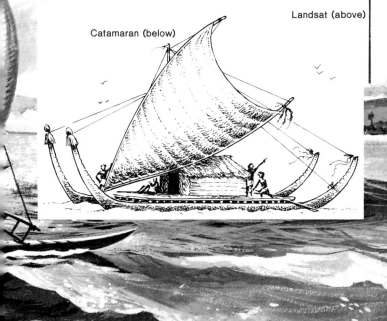

Strange Weather

Changing weather brings clouds, sunshine, wind, and rain. Unusual weather may cause strange effects. We see things that are not really there.

Mirages

Sometimes a layer of hot or cold air forms near the ground. It causes light rays to bend. Things seem to appear in the wrong places. When this happens it is called a *mirage*.

In dry, sunny deserts hot air may form just above the ground. Looking down at the hot layer, you see light rays from distant clouds that hit the layer. They bounce up to your eye so you see an image of the clouds upside down. They seem to be pools of water lying on the ground.

In cold areas, layers of icy air form above the ground. If you look through the cold air layer you see another kind of mirage. Light rays from the Sun bend downward as they pass through the cold layer. The Sun seems to be high in the sky when it is really below the horizon.

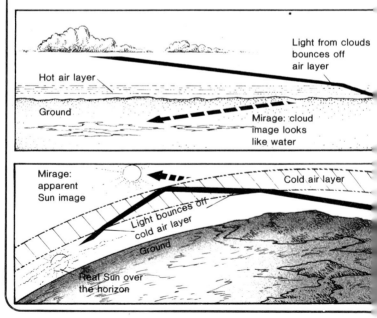

Light from clouds bounces off air layer

Hot air layer

Ground

Mirage: cloud image looks like water

Mirage: apparent Sun image

Cold air layer

Light bounces off cold air layer

Ground

Real Sun over the horizon

Hailstones

Water vapor sometimes forms balls of ice called hailstones. Most are as small as peas. But a few are huge.

The giant hailstone (right) weighed several pounds. It fell in the United States. The oddly shaped one below it fell in Australia.

Hailstorms sometimes ruin crops or smash roofs.

7½'' (190 mm)

1¾'' (45 mm)

Red Sunsets

In 1883 a volcano in Indonesia blew up. It was called Krakatoa. It blew up with such a bang that people heard it 3000 miles (4800 km) away. So much ash was hurled into the air that it blotted out the Sun. Darkness lasted for two days.

Black clouds of ash were flung 50 miles (80 km) high. These high clouds traveled around the Earth many times. All over the world there were bright red sunsets.

Krakatoa was quiet until 1927. Then a new volcano grew up from the ocean floor. It formed a small island nearby. The new island was named Anak Krakatoa—the ''child of Krakatoa.''

INFERIOR MIRAGE

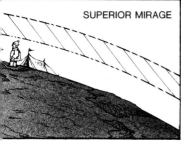

SUPERIOR MIRAGE

Lost Lands

In places, rising seas have drowned the land. The same thing can happen in other places if the sea is not kept out.

The Bering Bridge

Today North America and Asia are separated by the sea. But in the Stone Age, people could walk from one to the other. They could do this because the sea was much lower. A narrow neck of land connected North America and Asia. That vanished land is called the Bering Land-Bridge.

Atlantis

Greek legend tells of an island drowned by earthquakes. It was called Atlantis. Recently the remains of an ancient city have been found. It had been buried by volcanic ash on a small Greek island. This had once been part of a larger volcanic island—Santorini. Santorini blew up about 3400 years ago. Perhaps Santorini was once Atlantis.

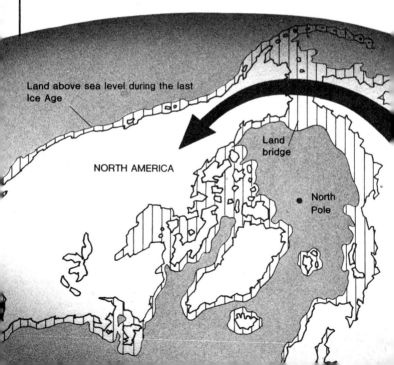

Land above sea level during the last Ice Age

NORTH AMERICA

Land bridge

North Pole

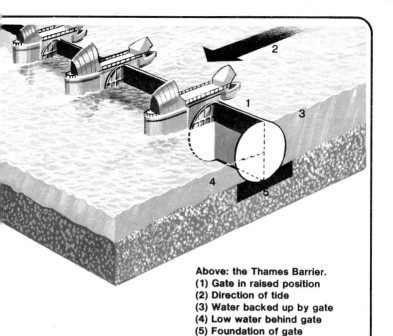

Above: the Thames Barrier.
(1) Gate in raised position
(2) Direction of tide
(3) Water backed up by gate
(4) Low water behind gate
(5) Foundation of gate

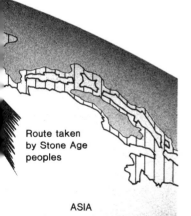

Route taken
by Stone Age
peoples

ASIA

London

London, England, is a city that is slowly sinking. It could be drowned someday by the River Thames. Engineers are trying to save it. They have built huge floodgates across the river. Someday a high tide may move upriver from the sea. But if it does, the floodgates will shut and keep the water out.

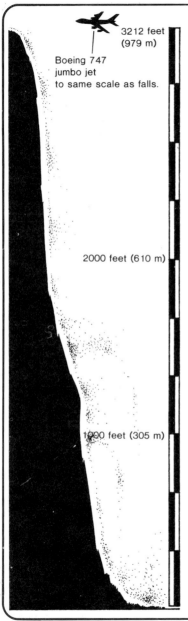

3212 feet
(979 m)

Boeing 747
jumbo jet
to same scale as falls.

2000 feet (610 m)

1000 feet (305 m)

Freshwater Wonders

More than 99 percent of the world's water is saltwater. But freshwater is often remarkable in its effects.

Angel Falls

In 1935 an American pilot was flying across Venezuela. He was forced to make a crash landing on a plateau. There he found a narrow river plunging over a cliff.

The waterfall proved to be the highest in the world. It is 3212 feet (979 m) high. That is

Left: Angel Falls, the world's highest waterfall, dwarfs a jumbo jet.

Venezuela

Angel Falls

SOUTH AMERICA

2½ times as high as the Empire State Building. It is called Angel Falls, after Jimmy Angel, the pilot who found it.

China's Sorrow

China's Hwang Ho river is sometimes called ''China's sorrow.'' Its floods have killed more people than any other natural disaster. Heavy rains make it burst its banks. It then floods the low plains around it. The worst flood of recent times was in 1931. Nearly four million people were drowned.

Vanished Lakes

Most lakes dry up in time. Many fill with mud. Others simply leak away. Lake Agassiz, in Canada, is one that leaked away.

This vast lake was almost as big as New Zealand. It was surrounded by mountains and a huge ice sheet. When the ice melted the water of the lake flowed away. Small parts of it still remain. They now form much smaller lakes such as Winnipegosis, Winnipeg, and Manitoba.

Ocean Wonders

There is always something new and amazing to be learned about the oceans.

A Shrinking Sea

In 1970 thick salt deposits were found beneath the Mediterranean Sea. Such deposits come from desert shores. It may mean that the Mediterranean was once much smaller and shallower than it is now.

Scientists have learned that there is a deep, rocky gorge far beneath the floor of the River Nile. This gorge is buried under nearly a thousand feet of mud. Long ago the Nile must have reached the Mediterranean by flowing through that gorge. This too seems to prove that the sea itself was once much lower.

Scientists now think that Africa and Spain were once

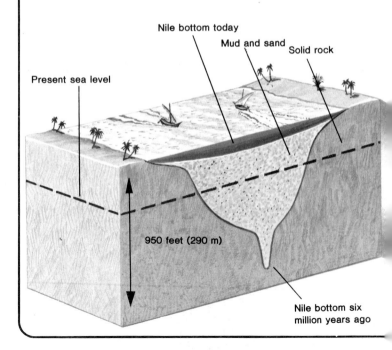

Present sea level

Nile bottom today

Mud and sand

Solid rock

950 feet (290 m)

Nile bottom six million years ago

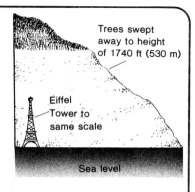

Trees swept away to height of 1740 ft (530 m)

Eiffel Tower to same scale

Sea level

joined. This cut off the Mediterranean from the ocean. Water stopped flowing in from the Atlantic. The Mediterranean nearly dried up.

The Coral Reef

One of nature's most astounding building jobs is the Great Barrier Reef of Australia. It is 1250 miles (2011 km) long and 500 feet (152 m) high. Yet tiny coral polyps built it.

Coral likes the warm, shallow waters of the South Pacific coast. There are many groups of these tiny sea creatures. Their hard, limy skeletons are the building blocks of the coral reef.

A Giant Wave

In 1958 there was a rock-slide in Alaska's Lituya Bay. Tons of rock slid into the sea.

This caused a huge wave. It was twice as high as the Eiffel Tower in Paris. The wave swept away about 4 square miles (10 km) of Alaskan trees and soil. Only bare rock was left behind.

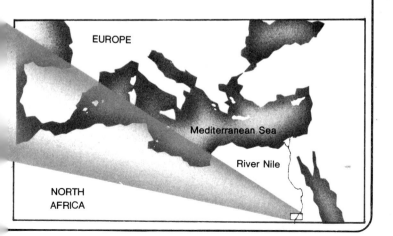

EUROPE

Mediterranean Sea

River Nile

NORTH AFRICA

Wanderers

Mountains, desert sands, and oceans stop the spread of many plants and animals. Yet living things have reached islands in mid-ocean. And there they have made their homes.

Monarchs

Millions of monarch butterflies head south from North America each year. Some of these beautiful creatures are blown far out to sea.

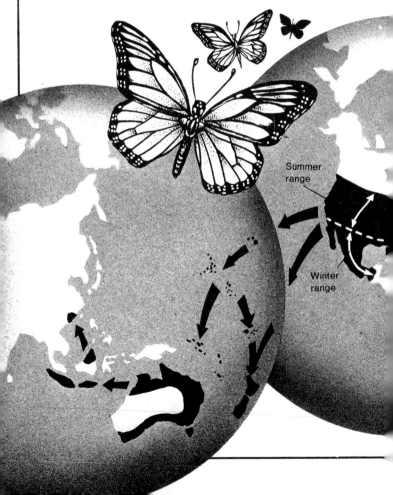

Summer range

Winter range

As the left-hand map shows, they may island-hop across the Pacific Ocean. They have reached Australia, Indonesia, and southern China.

Atlantic ocean winds blow other monarchs eastward. They are sometimes blown as far as the British Isles. Other butterflies have wound up in the Canaries—off the coast of North Africa.

Floating Zoos

Sometimes plants and animals are washed far out to sea on clumps of shrubs and grasses. These "rafts" were torn loose from river banks by floods.

Once a man fell asleep beside the river Congo. He woke up on a floating "island" far out in the ocean.

Most such travelers just drown. But a few land on islands in the sea. This is how lizards and tortoises arrived on the Galápagos Islands. These islands are four days' trip by modern ship from South America. Almost all of the land animals on the island of Madagascar floated in from Africa.

Drifting Coconuts

A few land plants actually use the sea. Its currents help them spread. Palm trees drop coconuts that fall into the sea. Currents can carry them for hundreds of miles. They are washed up on lonely island shores. Some of them sprout, and new trees start to grow along the beach.

Tomorrow's World

The world is always changing. Some changes are made by nature. Others are made by people. Tomorrow's world will be a different place from the one we know today.

Moving Icebergs
One day, tugs may tow icebergs from the Arctic to California. Some ice would melt on the way. But enough would last to supply huge amounts of cheap, fresh water to dry desert areas.

Hot or Cold
If the world's great ice sheets melt, the level of the seas will rise. All of the world's seaports and many major cities will be under water.

In the United States, all of Florida will disappear.

But if a new Ice Age begins, the level of the sea will fall. New areas of land will appear. Perhaps Asia and North America will again be connected by land. Some scientists think a new Ice Age may soon begin.

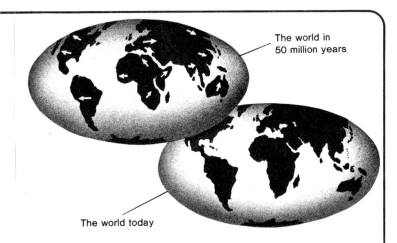

The world in 50 million years

The world today

Fifty Million Years From Now

Africa and South America are very slowly moving farther apart. This drift of the continents will continue. The map of the world will change. In fifty million years, Australia will have moved toward Indonesia. Africa may have split apart. The Americas will have drifted westward.

Index